This book is due for return on or before the last date shown below.

TABLE OF CONTENTS

PUBLISHERS NOTES

DEDICATION

This book is dedicated to those who suffer from smoking and those who seek freedom from smoking.

CHAPTER 1- A NEED OF WILLPOWER TO STOP SMOKING

Smokers do want to quit smoking and they are waiting for that auspicious day eagerly. But still quitting the smoking becomes impossible for them. They do try but again got caught in the same grip of an addiction. They want to get succeed but again find themselves standing on the same point from where they have started their journey for a good cause.

This does not happen with one or two smoker. It is a case with every other smoker. They are trying hard to quit it but are not capable because of the love for nicotine. Nicotine is a deadly drug but its addiction is very powerful. The fortunate thing is that thousands of people are successfully trying to escape its grip and many have already succeeded. They are same people who once have thought that they would not be able to quit. Finally they won over evil and turned their dream into the reality. Their determination has worked for them.

You can follow their footsteps too:

You need to fulfill the commitment you have done with yourself and with your near and dear ones. The first step you need to do some alterations in your thinking. Be optimist and change way of living a little. The activities you have associated with habit of smoking needs to have some modifications. Just change the way of dealing with them and you will notice a great change in you.

You need to associate a good reasoning behind cause of quitting and have to think about good consequences that follow. If you do not feel good about quitting, then you will never be able to quit smoking. You should be mentally as well as emotionally strong to escape this deadly danger.

If you properly condition yourself mentally then you can certainly come onto the commitment you have done with yourself. People are generally scared of the withdrawal effects without giving thought to their long term benefits. They never think that pleasures, comforts and enjoyment that they are getting from smoking is short term. These feelings exist at subconscious level. Studies say that we experience 60,000 thoughts a day. Unfortunately most people give rise to the negative ones in that percentage.

You must pen down what you think about smoking and its quitting. In general most people including smokers are against smoking. Things will start working effectively if you start applying what you say rather than what you feel.

CHAPTER 2- ADVANTAGES OF QUITTING SMOKING & DISADVANTAGES OF SMOKING

Do you know that around 1000 Americans are dying every day because of smoking?

One out of every six men is dying in United States because of smoking. It is quite clear now that smoking is one of the major causes of death. If you smoke then you are also enhancing the chances of diseases that will end up in death. The major diseases due to smoking are the coronary heart disease, lung cancer, mouth cancer and severe problems regarding throat, bladder, kidney and pancreas. Most of the diseases are so severe that there are no treatments available for them. The severe gangrene problem has been found in the Diabetic patients, who smoke a lot.

Now, this is the high time and you must quit smoking immediately. Do not think that it is impossible for you to quit it, as there are many chain smokers, who have quit smoking. The only thing one needs is the determination and once you achieve your destination then you will feel happy and contented.

Follow these rules and see the results:

Firstly, you need a firm determination of quitting this bad habit. When you have determined firmly, and then decide a date. Now, from this particular date, you will not touch the cigarette determine it firmly.

For a smoker, smoking is one of the essentials. Now you have decided to quit it and to attain the quitting, try some other work at the time of smoking.

As the date of quitting is approaching, try to minimize the intake of cigarettes and the conditions when you smoke. Take a glass jar, fill it with water and drop all the butts of cigarette into it.

Try to concentrate on the advantages after quitting cigarette, in your free time. You will find that quitting smoking have much more advantages than smoking. If one quit smoking then there will be considerable minimization in the risk involved due to heart disease, cancer and other deadly diseases. Earlier you use to get tired up easily, but now you have more power. You will also gain resistance from cough, cold and flu.

Quitting cigarette will also save the money, which you were burning to destroy your health. Put all the money you spend on your cigarette in the glass jar and in one month see your savings.

In the initial phases, nicotine will show its effects. It would be almost impossible for you to handle this temptation. However, try to divert your mind. You will also have to face a lot of problems like headache, irritation and coughing. All these are positive signs. To avoid them drink water, make your hands and mouth busy. Do not bother about them, as they will reduce with the time. During the initial phases of quitting smoking, you may feel anxiety. To get rid of anxiety does not take caffeine drinks, inhale deep breaths and go for walk. The best way to handle the problem is start-doing exercises.

Moreover, quantity of carbon monoxide in your blood will minimize and a considerable increment of oxygen. There will be glow at your face and your skin will turn pink. Your heartbeat will be normal and lungs become clearer.

Your risk to heart attack gradually decreases, if you are not smoking for a year or two.

To make it more interesting, look out for a friend interested in getting rid of it. Both of you can do wonders. Always try to avoid places that encourage smoking. After quitting, many people usually put on a lot of weight. To avoid this, go for an exercise program, eat healthy food and improve your way of living.

Some drugs can replace the harmful nicotine. But, it should not be taken without the advice of Doctor. For instance, Nicotine gum, Bupropion, Nicotine inhaler and Nicotine nasal spray. These drugs will surely helpful in quitting smoking.

Now, you have acquired your destination. It is the time to reward you for your achievement. Get that glass jar and you will be wondered to find the amount you have saved.

Many times, even after quitting people smoke. Do not think that your efforts have gone wasted. You should only consider the advantages of not smoking and start following the path of not smoking. The best thing one can do for quitting smoking is the faith in oneself. Have faith in yourself and you will attain the unachievable.

CHAPTER 3- EFFECT OF SMOKING ON MOTHER'S WOMB

Smoking is much dangerous for a pregnant woman than any other person. Smoking affects your unborn child. If you are going to plan your family or are already pregnant, then you need to concentrate on facts related to smoking. A Mother always wants to give a healthy and fit life to her baby. But continuing with your smoking are you really fulfilling your wish?

When you take a puff then the smoke that you inhale goes into your baby's body. It affects his weight resulting into less resistant body. Smoking affects his height too. Such babies whose mothers had smoked during their pregnancies are generally short in height. This possibility is much less in case of the women who smoke a full pack during pregnancy. At this stage even no physician suggests to continue this habit. Baby's body needs more supply of oxygen to survive in mother's womb. Supply of nicotine deprives a baby to consume his share of oxygen. Such children are not able to adjust socially than children of non-smoking mothers.

Studies show that the possibility of infant mortality is 50 percent higher when the mother smokes than in case of non -smoking mothers. Children of many smokers die of sudden infant death syndrome, or crib death. If pregnant women stop smoking by their fourth month of pregnancy then still they are out of danger zone.

Parenting is a tough job. If you do not sound well in your health then how will you be able to take care of your child? Most women suffer from lung cancer that is a deadly disease. A child always seeks for his mother's shelter. If you want to be there all time for your child, then you need to stop smoking at once.

Passive smokers are more prone to the diseases than chain smokers are. This applies on children also. As a matter of fact, they are too sensitive to problems raised by the passive smoking.

By quitting the smoking you are rendering a new life to your child. You and your child both will enjoy a healthy lifestyle. Quitting smoking is not an easy thing to do for the usual smokers. But alternatives will certainly work for you. There are many support centers that can help you out. Just enroll yourself in them. You can see your health care provider for solutions and suggestions. Your one step to quitting the smoking will lead your unborn to the path of a safe child.

CHAPTER 4- ALL ABOUT SMOKING

Some people are under misconception and take smoking as a hobby. According to recent studies conducted by AMA, American Lung and Heart Associations and the American Cancer society smoking is one of the main causes of premature death. Smoking means you are giving to yourself a slow poison treatment. Smoking does not only meteorites the smoker's health but it also affects the nearby standing person like your kids as their organs are on developing stage.

Smoking problem

It has become an accepted fact worldwide that cigarette smoking is the main agent of avoidable and premature death rate. It results in one in five deaths in United States. The data shows the deaths of over 400,000 people from 1995 to 1999 in U.S per year. Smoking acts as a catalyst in lung cancer, coronary heart diseases and chronic airway obstruction.

If we exclude adult deaths which is commonly a result of secondhand smoke, we see that both adult males and females have lost on an around 13 to14 years of their life expectancy. If this pace of consummation of tobacco goes on then approximately 6.4 million children will lose their lives prematurely. Economy has to endure the expenditure of over $100 billion in health care costs annually which results in loss of productivity including the death rate and medical expenses. Smoking has direct relation to the sources causing the lung cancer, emphysema and chronic bronchitis.

The primary cause of the death in U.S is cardiovascular disease which is again partially an outcome of the tobacco use. A survey shows the deaths of 65000 women who died of the lung cancer and 85000 men who died of lung and bronchus diseases. This shows that smoking is much injurious to health than the most people are aware about its harmful effects. This data should act as a statuary warning for people but instead of becoming aware they get back to the same habit again.

Some people do want to quit smoking and some even tries to make an attempt which is good starting for a good cause as done in 2001 by many people but to increase this figure it is essential that the victims should be encourage so that he may get counted in the list of successful.

CHAPTER 5- BELIEVE IN FACTS

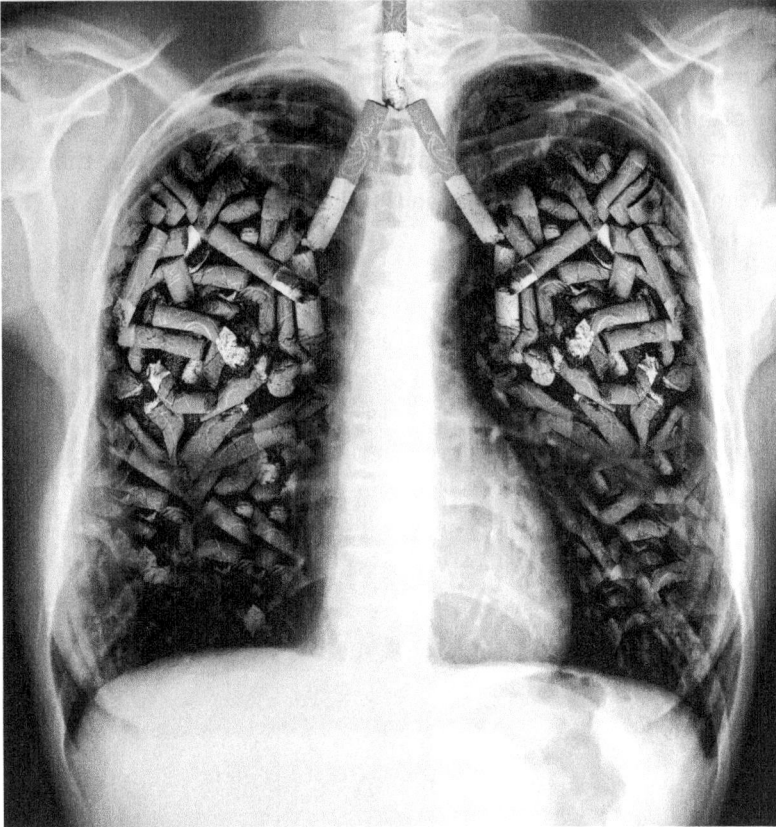

Everything in this world is made for a purpose, so do the tobacco. Tobacco serves several medicinal purposes, but its wrong use has created more wrong than right. We human beings are responsible in converting the blessings of God into a Curse.

We often read in newspaper, serious warnings from health ministry about the hazards of smoking. For instance, smokers die young as compare to non-smokers. Instead of these warnings, there is a considerable increment in the number of smokers.

A recent survey has shown increment in production, sale and the number of smokers in Nigeria. Along with it, there is also an increment in the death rate due to smoking.

A survey conducted reveals the growth in the number of death of passive smokers. In a year, more than 11,000 people die in UK due to passive smoking. You can conclude, if this is the data of passive smoker then what about the smokers.

In public places, health experts and Doctors are demanding complete ban on smoking. Due to growing death rate of passive smokers, they are demanding certain rules and regulations for their protection.

There are several causes of death such as household structure, unemployment, passive smoking and active smoking. On the base of researches done over the causes of death, it has been found that smoking is the main cause.

Tobacco one of the main ingredients of smoking is already causing a lot of harm. But, still its producers are making a lot of money from its farming. Tobacco is nothing but death of our loved ones; still we love to have it. We are spending a lot of money in buying this poison. Over the cigarette pack, it is clearly written that 'Cigarette smoking is injurious to health'. Still we go for it and the cigarette companies are making a lot of money from our death.

When all of us know, that cigarette smoking is dangerous and harmful for health then why do not we quit it. A few significant steps are also needed from the side of the government. They need to ban all the products related to addiction such as cocaine, heroin, Indian hemp etc.

Moreover, we also need a powerful determination of quitting smoking. Based on a few misconceptions, we should not make a fool of ourselves that we cannot quit. Make your mind clear from all the wrong beliefs and determine that 'I will never smoke'.

Chapter 6- Can Quitting The Final Cigarette Be A Bliss?

We always think what will happen after giving up bad habits? Let us analyze it thoroughly in case of smoking. The benefits that follow are according to the timeline before which the smoker has quitted smoking like:

What happens after 20 minutes giving up smoking?

Smoking always results in high blood pressure which is harmful for heart as it increases the danger of heart attack. But the minute we give up this habit, the risk minimizes and blood pressure rate becomes normal.

The next is after 10 hours:

The level of carbon monoxide becomes half after 10 hours of giving smoking. It is one of the major pollutants that produce ill effects on cognitive skills and health and oxygen is one of the most vital substances which are necessary for survival. High level of carbon monoxide decreases intake of blood from lungs which can give birth to serious problems.

We increase our energy levels by smoothing the passage of oxygen as we curtail the level of carbon monoxide by quitting smoking.

Let us next analyze what happens after 24 hours of quitting smoking;

Not smoking for 24 hours is a marvelous starting for the chain smokers that provides them strong bearing power, less level of fatigue after exercise and quick recovery.

Moving to 48 hours from one whole day gives new experience to person as nicotine is removed from their body which earlier has resulted in bad side effects by causing vomiting, stomachache and it also enhances the possibility of hypothermia.

What happens after 2-22 weeks?

Person gets rid of bad circulation and also of numerous other problems like slow skin healing, cold feet, Raynaud's disease and peripheral vascular disease (PVT).

What happens after 1 year?

According to the studies conducted in U.K, smoking results in around 20,000 deaths due to cardiovascular diseases. Quitting smoking for 1 year reduces the risk of heart attack to half.

What happens after 10 years?

After minimizing the danger of heart attack our good habit of quitting smoking results in reducing the danger of lung cancer to half. In 1999, most of cancer death was due to lung cancer which was in return an outcome of the smoking.

What happens after 15 years?

After this much of the time period person who once was chain smoker leads a healthy life as a normal man who has never smoked. At last the good habit has repaid back.

CHAPTER 7- HABITS CAN BE DANGEROUS

Many people are well aware of disadvantages that are caused by smoking, still smoking is a problem. Few of them are able to give up the habit. Studies show that reason behind is myth of addictions.

Addicts love nicotine and think it is not allowing them to quit smoking. It is a physiological addiction. The physical suffering intensifies if body has to wait for the fix it is longing for irrespective of the fact whether person is awakened or sleeping. People of UK holidaying in Canada always prefer to keep a pack of cigarette with them to resist the long journey of around 10-12 hours. On choosing holiday destinations according to flight length they choose pack of cigarette. But their body has to forget smoking only for the flight duration.

There are many chain smokers who smoke 30 cigarettes a day not because of their body craving for nicotine but because they have become habitual. They need it to satisfy their habit.

Heroine addicts are the worst sufferers. They have to indulge themselves in crimes like robbery, stealing because they have not got the cash to fulfill their body longing. Under certain circumstances some people has to go for smoking and once you inject this habit in yourself, it becomes passion for you. This is what clinical addiction does and tobacco manufacturers take advantage of this blaming entirely to habits.

An interesting reality is that when we continue smoking the effect of drug lessens but arouses a psychological need for more doses to increase effects. This is how; we become mere puppets of our own body.

Smoking is a problem of mind and not of body. It is not an easy habit to get rid of. If we can make our body understand to quit habit in flight hours then why cannot we make it understand it at other events?

The answer is habit has an environmental trigger. It switches on picking up the phone, on sitting in car, after meals etc.   Smokers think that smoking gives them pleasure. Studies show that quitting smoking is an easy task. Hypnotherapy is an effective means by which people can quit smoking easily.

A smoker is just as a driver of a car whop always presses the brakes whenever any car comes in front of his car irrespective of the fact that his own car is not started. This happens because of habit. Quitting habit is much difficult than quitting anything else.

CHAPTER 8- DO YOU STILL WANT TO SMOKE AFTER ALL THESE FACTS?

Necessity For Expecting mothers

God has bestowed all His blessing on Mother by giving her a chance to nurture one more life in her body .Then why they want to become life snatchers to their child only for the sake of a bad habit?

Expecting mothers should at once stop smoking as it can prove very dangerous for your unborn. It is vital to quit this worst habit prior knowing about pregnancy as well as during pregnancy. Consummation of alcohol and smoking contaminates baby food due to which the risk of birth defects is more. A little carelessness can result in irreparable losses. Timely care will definitely help to get rid of worries. A visit to health care is must at this stage. No physician prescribes to continue habit of consuming alcohol so it becomes all more necessary to quit this habit.

Bestowing a safe life to the baby is responsibility that falls on shoulder of mother. Would be mothers must be aware of the facts relating to healthy stay of their child. Women who continue to smoke during pregnancy are literally giving a slow poison treatment to themselves as well as to their baby.. Smoking affects your unborn fetus resulting in various respiratory defects in child later on in his life stages. When baby is in mother's womb, his body parts are attached to his mother parts. Anything which mother eats goes directly in baby's body. When a pregnant woman smokes then baby gets less oxygen than he usually would. We all know oxygen is the most vital thing to ensure survival. But smoking deprives the child of a healthy stay. Less supply of oxygen results in irregular development of baby body parts and also contributes to preterm labor, hence is threatening to his life.

Consulting a physician:

At this stage it is essential for you to pay a visit to your health care provider.

Your physician will design a time table for you that would be feasible and easy to adopt. Following the prescribed schedule you will be able to quit your unhealthy habits ensuring a safe life to your child. There are many helping aids available for expecting mothers which help efficiently at this trying time. Work out classes is also given by these support groups which lessens your stress. Timely taking up better things will provide your unborn child a safe delivery and a healthy life.

CHAPTER 9- DO YOU WANT TO FREE YOURSELF FROM HEART DISEASES?

If the answer is yes, then follow the following steps to minimize the risk of heart attack:

1. Take out time to relax and do proper exercises. Cardiovascular exercise is must for people who have already experienced heart attack. Exercise not only reduces the risk of heart attack, it also relives us of tiresome schedule by making us stress free.

2. Be optimist. Never give yourself to despair. Ensure that living unhealthy and unhealthy thinking is one of the main causes of the heart disease. After nurturing positive hopes we will start feeling good about ourselves as well as relieved. You will find yourself on top of the world. Feel yourself enjoying everything.

3. Take balanced diet, full of green leafy vegetables and pulses and drink 8 to 10 glasses of water every day.

4. Try to associate yourself more with the good habits that determine quality of life and improve lifestyle. Do not take the initiative fast. Slowly try to abstain yourself from bad habits. Healthy habits bring ecstasy, health and make life a pleasant experience.

5. Quitting the worst habit smoking is an essential step to save yourself from the risk of heart attack. Smoking contains nicotine which fills laziness in us and makes us addicted to cigarette. By continuing smoking we are shortening our lifespan. Quitting smoking will help us to take physical fitness regimen. You can start with slow walking, deep breathing as well as cycling. Gradually you will get into habit of a proper exercising schedule.

6. Everyone has room for temptations. One must learn to control temptations and longings for bad habits. If once we learn the art of controlling cravings then we will surely ensure our healthy stay.

7. Discover your own ways to enjoy yourself. Laugh whole heartedly. Laughter is an abundantly available medicine that increases the life span and moreover it is natural, free and does not have any side effect so why not to get it?

8. Avoid eating fried and junk snacks and also the food that contains saturated fats. This food stuff increases the cholesterol level in blood. Higher cholesterol is again a symptom of heart attack.

9. In drinks try to avoid red wine, alcohol. These are detrimental to our health.

10. Avoid spicy food. Eating healthy diet helps us to control our carbohydrates, fats and blood pressure.

Chapter 10- Does Smoking Rob You Of Your Facial Charm?

Good and healthy skin is one thing that everyone wants to have. Skin originates from within. The food that we eat gets broken into simpler substances and nutrients. These nutrients and oxygen get mix with blood and are transported to all our body parts through thousands of bloodstreams. Larger parts of these nutrients get absorbed by the skin which is essential for healthy stay of our body cells.

Internal health and external beauty are two sides of the same coin. We get oxygen naturally through our breathing but smoking results in inhaling of harmful carbon monoxide. Cigarettes not only contain carbon monoxide but also contain poisonous gases like ammonia, butane, nicotine, carbolic acid, formic aldehyde, prussic acid, pyridine, parvoline, arsenic and cadmium. Carbon monoxide, the most intoxicated gas mixes with the hemoglobin present in the blood. Our blood cells absorb carbon monoxide gas much faster than oxygen. In this way carbon monoxide displaces oxygen in large quantity depriving our skin cells of their healthy life. Skin and smoking are inversely related with each other.

Skin has its own repairing system. Smoking destroys its natural system and results in premature aging. At this stage skin loses its natural glow and charm and develops a pale look.

These outcomes on the skin are catastrophic. Smoking deprives skin of vitamin C which is an essential vitamin. Moreover it is an unstable vitamin and cannot be produce by body. Vitamin C helps the skin inn generating new healthy cells giving the skin a youthful look. Breaking of the collagen results in wrinkles.

You have often noticed that chain smokers usually have sunken eyes and dark circles around their eyes. It is because smoking damages the cells making it scaly and causing wrinkles. It does show its effect on lips also making the lips black and robbing them of their natural appearance.

People spent much money on cigarettes and tobacco which gives them nothing but diseases and side effects. Each one of us know that smoking is injurious to health still we are not able to favour our self by quitting our worst habit.. Instead of depriving our self of healthy and natural glow, we can spend that much amount on facials and good skin rejuvenators. Taking a balanced diet, rich in fibers help in elimination of wastes resulting in healthy skin.

CHAPTER 11- EDUCATE YOUR CHILD ON SMOKING

Studies show adults can quit smoking under care of a counselor and physician. But this possibility is next to impossible with teenagers. Pre- teen age is an age in which we want to gain each and every experience whether good or bad. Our habits start forming at this stage like smoking. Most of us take first puff only to boast it about to our friends and later on it becomes a harmful habit. Some steps can help parents to ensure safety of their child:

1. Generally a child learns from the habits of his parents. If you are a smoker then the foremost step needs to be taken by you. Get yourself free from the smoking habit and try to figure out the bad effects of smoking in front of your child. If a child sees his parents using good manners like eating healthy food then he is likely to follow those good habits. On the contrary if he sees his parents smoking, he surely takes up that. Only verbal explanation would not help. You have to practically put them.

2. Talk to your kids. You can start with explaining them functions of heart and lungs and how bad habits harm their smooth functioning. Insert a mental picture of the outcomes. Instead of praising the smoking trend, try to criticize actors who smoke in movies and T.V programs. Make sure you do that in front of your kids.

3. Tell him about the harmful effects that smoking leads to like it blocks the bloodstreams, robs the face charm, causes pale look. Try to encourage kids more abut good habits by telling them about its consequences like healthy skin, active body, physical fitness.

4. Help your child to get involve in the activities in which they are interested. A child should learn to develop an optimist

point of view towards life. Encourage them to make good friends and not to get involve in bad company. Appreciate your youngsters on their good deeds and also not forget to scold them on their bad ones. Do not pamper them. Your child should be able to judge between right and wrong so they are able to say no to their bad habits when the trying time   comes.

5. Spend some good time with your ward. Be aware of your child activities. Talk to him about different topics. Start with asking him how he spent his day. All you need is the tact to handle your kid with care.

Chapter 12- Enjoy Life After Quitting Smoking

Are you aware of the consequences of smoking?

Smoking exposes you to several deadly diseases like cancer, asthma and heart problems. Your near and dear ones are also being exposed to these diseases along with you. Thus, for the sake of health of your loved ones you must quit smoking.

If you are quitting smoking that means, you are giving way to healthy and fresh life. Moreover, there are certain sudden changes you will experience after quitting smoking.

These are mainly positive changes and you will only benefit from them. When you quit smoking then within eight hours, the amount of carbon monoxide gas will be normal. Due to excessive smoking, the content of carbon monoxide gas in the blood enhances. But, the moment you quit smoking it becomes normal.

The chances of heart attack also reduce within 24 hours. Do not forget the money that you were burning while smoking. Quitting smoking means instant saving. Make it a routine of keeping the money that you use for buying cigarettes into a jar. After a month, check your jar and enjoy the achievement.

After two or three months, you will experience more benefits of quitting smoking.

You will be much healthier. The lung will function much better and its functioning will increment by 30 percent. After one year, the chances of heart diseases will reduce to half. Moreover, the risk of death due to lung cancer will also decrease.

You can enjoy several other benefits by quitting smoking. You are also saving your children from acquiring deadly diseases. If a pregnant woman is a smoker then she is exposing her baby to several deadly chemicals. These deadly chemicals will harm the baby a lot. The baby will weigh lower than the normal babies will; organs will be of smaller size and more chances of taking up tobacco. Such babies will never be able to lead a healthy and active life. Thus, for the sake of your baby's health you must quit smoking. If a pregnant woman quit smoking then she is blessing life to her baby.

All it need is a decision from you. Your determination of quitting smoking guarantees healthy future for you. You will feel active. There will be glow at your face. Earlier you were having pale yellow fingernails. Now, you can see the difference.

Then, why do not you enjoy all these benefits of quitting smoking?

Thus, the decision is in your hands.

Chapter 13- Exercising: A Friend For Whole Life

Can you define a friend? One who is always there with you in difficulties and make your life beautiful and enjoyable. We are having a lot of friend, but there is one person who gives you more than a friend. She is none other than our, Mother. Mother, this very word when we listen or say, gives us relief as we are sitting in the comforts of home. She is the one, who takes care of everyone in the house and makes life and things easier for us. She is the one, whom we could say a caregiver.

Hey! What is this caregiver?

Caregiver is the one, who always helps you, when you are in trouble and take care of your wants. But, who takes care of the mom? She also gets tired or her muscles get fatigued. For all the moms out there, apart from doing household jobs and taking care of your family members, you should also take care of your health. Mothers are the backbone of a good home, so all of you must take care of yourself. If you spend a little time on exercise from your daily routine, then surely, you can give more to your family members than they demand. Exercise will give you more energy, flexibility to your body and power to do work. After exercising, there will be a feeling of freshness and you can do work, more efficiently. It is also prevent you from getting fatigued. Sometimes, one may get the frustrated with the same regular job. Exercising makes you fresh and act as an exit door for every frustration and all.

Apart from making you mentally fresh and emotionally strong, it also has many benefits regarding your health. It is quite helpful in minimizing the ratio of heart problems, diabetes and obesity. It also enhances the levels of blood pressure, prevents osteoporosis, provide balance to your body while climbing stairs or walking. Lastly, the one thing, which every woman in the world wants to maintain, is her beauty. Exercising regularly will bring glow and freshness at your face. The cause of this radiant complexion is the inner freshness that you are experiencing.

Getting started

There must be many questions or excuses in your mind regarding exercises.

For Instance, I am too busy to do all these things, or how could I exercise at such an age? On the other hand, where should I exercise?

Do not worry; there is a solution of each of your query. First, you can take out some time for exercise, from your daily work easily. There are easy exercises that you can perform without any need of extra time. Such, as gardening, going for short walks in the evening, housework or if possible then you can also join a club.

Second thing one must consider before joining any exercise program is the proper medical checkup. You must consult your family physician or any other doctor, before going for an exercise program. Get all your tests done, such as the blood or ECG etc. Due to any complication in your tests, if your doctor advises you not to do exercise then simply follow your doctor's advice. On the other hand, if he says you are perfectly fit then you should definitely follow this exercise program.

There is one question in your mind, which is disturbing you a lot. Who will take care of the small baby, or old grandmother, or any other family member, who is unwell? To solve this problem, call an agency or your family members can help you out or any of your friends. Thus, you need a proper planning to overcome the problem.

Now, you are ready to follow this program, but still one question is disturbing you. You are concerned about your safety. It may be possible that you will get hurt or seriously injured. To avoid such situations, always appoint a trainer or a buy a book or video CD, sport shoes etc.

Plan exercise program for you

The best exercise program one can follow is under the guidance of a trainer. In your staring phases, never exercise too hard. According to your MHR (maximum heart rate), one should exercise at 70 to 80 percent of heart rate.

The different types of exercises are:

1. Aerobic- This involves walking, swimming, dancing etc. All muscle related activities.

2. Weight training-It enhances the muscle power and balance of the body.

3. Warm up exercises minimizes the chance of injury. Pursue warm up exercises before performing the exercise program. On your fitness level, maintain your THR for 20 to 60 minutes.

4. To avoid dizziness, you should end with five minutes of cool down exercises.

Within the periods of two to six months, you will surely feel some change in you. Thus, to lead a healthy life, continue this program throughout your life.

CHAPTER 14- EXPECTING MOTHERS SHOULD QUIT SMOKING

All mothers-to-be, who are waiting for their babies desperately, must take care if they are smokers. Your only priority is the unborn baby and you must be attentive regarding his health. The first thing you can do for your baby is to quit smoking. Several problems can arise to your baby because of your smoking habits. The unborn baby is at maximum danger of many kinds of diseases because of your smoking habit. Every mother wants a healthy baby. But, your smoking habit will never fulfill your wish and it may harm your baby. Statistics show the considerable increment of smoking among women in United States.

The woman who is a chain smoker, when she decides to have a baby or when she is already expecting, should immediately quit smoking. Quitting smoking will prove to be beneficial for you as well as your baby. If a woman wants to quit smoking then pregnancy is the best period to quit it. It is the time, when your only priority is the baby and it would be easier for you to quit it. During the early period of pregnancy, it would be tough for you to quit smoking and you feel unwell. However, at the same time it would be easier to quit also, as it will not taste well to you.

Regarding baby's health, if you quit smoking before conceiving then it would be much beneficial. During pregnancy, your body should have no nicotine, as it will narrow down the blood vessels. The blood vessels that are contracted because of nicotine, also includes the placenta and the baby. It will be better for your baby, if you even avoid any other replacement of nicotine, such as patch or gum. All these things are a little tough to you. But, if you make yourself mentally strong and do certain planning, then definitely you are going to quit it. A smoker woman if quits before conceiving then the weight of the baby will be same as of the non-smoker woman's baby. Moreover, if a smoker woman quits smoking during the initial phases of pregnancy then your baby will be quite normal and you are saving him from many severe diseases.

After the birth of baby, do not start smoking again. The baby is always closer to the mother and indirectly you are passing all the bad effects of smoke into him. So, never think that it is too late now to quit. Whenever you feel that, I must quit now that is the best time to quit.

Some deadly diseases, which you are passing to your baby directly, but unknowingly:

Abruption is caused because of nicotine that at an early period separates fetus from placenta. This could also result in the death of the baby.

Vasoconstriction is the narrowing of the blood vessels, which are carrying food and oxygen to the baby. It also damages the placenta, which is actually a link between mother and the baby. Due to smoking of the mother, baby weighs less than the normal baby does.

Your smoking habit will also degrade your child performance in school. There is the danger of leukemia, due to mother's smoking habit. There are also dangers of attack of pediatric asthma and other kinds of allergies to the baby. There are also several cases of Infant death due to smoking mother.

In spite of such a long list of bad effects on the baby, if the mother still prefers to smoke then you must be ashamed of yourself. Your smoking habit is killing you and your baby. So, determine to quit smoking and bless your child with healthy and long life.

CHAPTER 15- GETTING FAMILIAR WITH HOW SMOKING WORKS

You know that with each puff of a cigarette, you send a definite amount of nicotine to your brain. Nicotine is a quick acting drug than heroine. It injects addiction into the veins. When a person begins his cigarette, the level of blood goes down to half within the time limit of half an hour and more than half within an hour.

Smoker suffers different symptoms after extinguishing his puff as the nicotine starts to leave the blood stream quickly. The restless feeling starts overpowering his mind arousing a desire to have one more cigarette. To satisfy his longing he puffs more and for 5-6 minutes, the craving ends. In this way smoker gets the fresh supply of nicotine. This is not the end. The mechanism is like a vicious circle, a never ending process. We need to break this chain but again the question arises HOW?

It is our mistake that we take nicotine for an order that has to carry out. Actually it is nothing but a monster which requests its food after every minute. We do not need to obey it all the time. But still we do. It can be term as a panic which after some time sends message to the brain to demand more of it. Puffing smoke, we expose ourselves to thousands of harmful chemicals, some of which causes cancer. Smoking also increases our heart beat rate. Smoker soon gets prone to different cancers than a non-smoker does.

Studies show women who smokes are 20 times more prone to cancer than men are. Breast cancer is one of the worst forms of cancer that generally makes women its victim.

Smokers have to bear the pain of heart attack as the smoke which they inhale blocks the heart veins. Blockage of vein results in fast supply of blood and ultimately an attack.

A severe attack sometimes results into death. Finally we become food of the monster. We can do everything to save ourselves but still we are incapable of escaping. There are so many ways which can help us a lot like exercise, taking a nutritious diet rich in fibers that helps in elimination of wastes. We awake when we come face to face with the problem and that delay causes us to suffer whole life.

CHAPTER 16- GOOD BYE SMOKING

After a long time, you have finally decided to say good-bye to smoking. Good-bye to smoking means, a complete change in your way of living. Now, your first job is to bring a change in your normal routine.

You need to develop a brand new atmosphere for you. Developing a new atmosphere is also a part of exercise in quitting smoking. Make everything around you such that it will give a fresh feeling to you. For Instance, if you often smoke near the telephone then change its place.

Set a new timetable for you. Include the visit to gym in your daily routine. If going to gym is not possible then go for a morning walk or jog. This is the healthiest way for the beginning of the day.

Take care that getting started is easy, but making it a routine is a little tough.

People often begin in a great way, such as buying tracksuits, gym wear or running shoes and enjoy a lot the earlier days in gym. But, as the time passes they take it as a burden and find it difficult to manage their time for gym.

There is a common mistake done by most of us. We go to gym, in evening. In evening, we are completely tired and no more enthusiasm is left on us. So, it would be beneficial to go the gym in the morning. In the morning, we are fresh after a long rest. Secondly, exercise enhances the flow of blood in the body and gives us more energy. Moreover, our exercise program will not effect in the morning and we can make plan for the day.

Fresher should do exercise under the expert guidance. A professional trainer is must for a proper start. One can also go for a few simple exercises that do not need any trainer. Swimming and walking are also the best form of exercises. You only need to get up early in the morning and enjoy the fresh and pollution-less city.

Go for tea instead of coffee, clean your houses and try to divert from everything that reminds you of smoking.

Do something interesting in evening, but take care not to play on money. Create a list of those things that stresses you and try to avoid them completely. Never make excuses for smoking. For instance, stress is the most common excuse. But you can de-stress yourself by doing something more creative such as breathing exercises or meditating.

Thus, apply these steps in your routine and say good-bye to smoking.

CHAPTER 17- HANDLING THE PAIN

When you ask smokers the cause for their smoking, their instant reply will be to de-stress. Suppose your three-year-old toddler is crying for a toy. How would you react? You will give him the toy, leave him, or give him some drugs to keep him calm. Similarly, your child is anxious about the coming torment. In order to calm him down, you will advise him, or give him some kind of drugs.

In all the above said examples, the child is suffering from some kind of pain or anxiety. You can control the temper of your child by a little advise, support and assurance. The cause for their anxiety is the demands during the development phase. When we grow physically, emotionally, academically or spiritually, we experiences anxiety. We should never take our growing phase as burden. All of us have the tendency to become sad or feeling pain or anxiety. But, we must try to overcome this attitude. We can never be happy without this growth. Growth plays significant part for our contentment and happiness.

We can never introduce our child to this deadly addiction, as we are well aware of its consequences. Do you think it is good to smoke for attaining relief?

Smokers make several excuses for smoking. For Instance, feeling lonely or having a lot of job stress. One of the several common excuses of smoker is that there is no fun in social gathering without smoking. This clearly shows that smokers make excuses to smoke. They smoke in stress as well as fun.

Women often say that quitting smoking means putting a lot of weight. Do you think it is a justified cause to smoke?

Smokers are well aware that smoking is injurious. Thus, to divert their minds they make such excuses. The cause for these false excuses is the addiction of nicotine.

Once you quit the smoking habit, you will realize that smoking only harms. It does not help you from overcoming the stress. But, it is the cause for several deadly diseases. Even after quitting smoking, you may tempt to have a cigarette. You may be tempted at social gatherings or feeling lonely or sad. Before taking cigarette, remember that smoking is nothing but killing oneself. It never helps you. It only harms you and makes you weak.

Whenever you want to smoke, just give a few seconds to yourself. You will realize the blunder, you are about to commit.

CHAPTER 18- HOOKAH: SMOKING EQUIPMENT

Smoking a Hookah is a very slow and comfortable experience of smoking. Smoking hookah demands a little preparation. You need to prepare tobacco. It is not similar to nicotine addiction or the puff of cigarette. But, it is like relaxing among your friends. People continue to smoke hookah for 30 to 60 minutes.

The preparation for Hookah smoking goes like this. Firstly, cleaning of Hookah is done with cold water. Then select a bowl of tobacco, light it and add charcoal to it. The aroma of hookah will come out through the bubbling water. After filtering it with water, it becomes cool and soft. The pleasant smoke of hookah will charge up the senses.

Certain techniques are also applied to enhance the experience of hookah smoking, such as putting ice in the water or chilling of the hoses. Addition of fruit juice or wine in the water leads to enhance the flavor of hookah smoke. To develop a special flavor, customers as well as the manufacturers mix tobacco with other flavors.

But, before smoking Hookah take these precautions and steps. Charcoal used in the Hookah should be appropriate, as there are certain harmful charcoal briquettes that can lead to intake of carbon monoxide, a poisonous gas. Take a little quantity of Hookah tobacco in the bowl. Some people add more tobacco to enhance the flavor of Hookah, but it is a wrong notion. If you are not getting the desired flavor then it is because of less heated coals. Add more fresh and hot coals and enjoy flavor of Hookah smoking.

Hookah smoking is mostly done among friends and family members. It is more or less like a culture or tradition. Thus, Hookah smoking has certain rules and regulations. For Instance, Charcoal heat should never be utilized for lighting cigarettes. On another person's face, never blow smoke. But, if the person demands and want to enjoy the flavor then you can blow the smoke. Never share the plastic mouthpiece with other person. When a person set a hose on the table that means he had finished smoking. Now, other person can use the hose. Wrap the hoses around the stem, after the completion of hookah smoking. While smoking hookah only go for tobacco.

So, enjoy the Hookah smoking with your friends.

CHAPTER 19- HOW NON-SMOKERS GET BREAST CANCER

Some people have taken smoking for fashion but this trend of theirs can lead them at the threshold of most ugly form of cancer- Breast cancer. The studies and researches draw a line between truth and myth. One of existing misconceptions is the myth that young men generally get addicted fast to smoking. But it has been found that young women adapt this bad habit much quickly than young men. The next horrid conclusion that comes forward is that passive smoker is at high risk of breast cancer than chain smokers.

World health organization shows us the true picture of smoking by associating it with 25 cancers like uterine, kidneys, cervix, and pancreas. Women and non-smoker are finding more prone to the breast cancer than any other form of cancer and unfortunately sufferers' list is going high day by day. It proves that smoking is not only deteriorating chain smoker health but also showing its side effects on health of persons standing nearby him. For women, smoking is synonym of death as it enhances the risk of heart strokes and heart attacks making them the worst victim and the chances get tenfold if they are using medicines for birth control along with smoking.

List of ill effects produced by smoking never ends making it a never ending process. Smoker take cigarette happily thinking that it will free them of tensions and stress but it releases them of their life. Dull look is easily visible on face. They soon develop wrinkles. They suffer of bad breath and yellow teeth and are ever complaining about tongue and stomach ulcers.

Children adopt bad habit more quickly than elders do. Parents who smoke inspire their wards to follow their black footsteps by their wrong habit and setting wrong example for them. Children of such parents can never differentiate between good and bad because from their initial developing stage they have only seen bad deeds.

Smoking blocks person thinking capacity. It makes one so much addicted that for every tense stage in life he needs its help.

CHAPTER 20- HOW TO QUIT SMOKING WITH WATER THERAPY

Like they say, it is easier said than done. Likewise, it is easy to admonish someone who smokes, or to ask him to quit the habit. Ask someone, who has quit smoking, how hard it had been for him/her. The reply you get will help you understand the almost super-human effort that goes into the entire process of quitting the habit.

The urge to smoke that one last cigarette is always there with people who have already quit the habit. People who have quit active smoking for years report to have had those occasional urges to smoke. Unfortunately, many, who after having successfully quitted the habit, get back to smoking just because they could not hold back the temptation of smoking that occasional cigarette their friend offered. There is no point getting back to square one after what a smoker goes through to quit smoking in the first place. Those occasional urges need to be controlled strongly.

Thankfully, smokers can opt for a very simple and inexpensive way out of this dilemma. Water is said to help people get out of their craving for a smoke. The good news is that it is helping fresh quitters during the initial weeks. People who have been smoking for a long time get used to nicotine, a strong drug. When a person quits smoking or is in the gradual process of quitting, the body craves for nicotine it is used to having on an everyday basis. Nicotine needs to be flushed out of the system, which water can do rather effectively. The more the water consumption, the more is the elimination of toxins. On an average, a person who has that urge to smoke should double his intake of water. What is thought more practical is a gradual reduction in the number of cigarettes a person smokes. That way the body gets used to the lesser intake of nicotine on an ongoing basis. Sudden quitting upsets the body and the resultant craving can create more withdrawal symptoms. Headaches are one of the common symptoms of withdrawal.

If you have quit smoking, but gave in to the urge, do not feel guilty. All you need to do is gulp down 3 or 4 glasses of water to flush out the toxins you introduced to the body. Make a fresh resolution not to give into the urge again. When the urge is on, remember not to give in to it. Instead, drink a few glasses of water reminding yourself not to add more toxins to your system.

Chapter 21 - Hypnosis: The Best Way To Stop Smoking

Smokers, who are getting aware of the possible health hazards and want to quit smoke at any cost, need not worry. There are several options for them. All of us know that smoking is nothing but addiction of nicotine. There are several companies manufacturing pills or nicotine replacement patches. These nicotine replacement pills are quite helpful in quitting smoking. Apart from these pills, there is one more option for quitting this addiction of nicotine. It is Hypnosis!

Most of the smokers stop smoking for some time after using these products. However, after sometime they start smoking again. The cause for again taking up smoking is that they were always conscious of having replacement pills for smoking. This means they were always conscious that smoking provides them something. Thus, the desire to smoke still exists in them. On the other hand, Hypnosis completely changes the attitude of smoker towards smoking. It put an end to the inner desire of the smoker for smoking. Once the smoker put an end to his inner desire for smoking, then he will never take up the cigarette again.

If you are a little health conscious then you can understand the importance of Hypnosis rather than nicotine replacement pills. The cause of your quitting smoking is that you want your body to be healthy, free from all kinds of toxins. However, nicotine is still getting entry into your body through the intake of these pills. So, consider Hypnosis rather than pills.

Duration taken by Hypnosis to quit smoking is quite shorter than the replacement pills. You would be astonished to know that Hypnosis takes only one hour or less to quit smoking completely. On the other hand, these replacement pills take many weeks.

In US, from your taxes you can remove the cost of programs that you have attended for quitting smoking. The cost of these programs can be added in the medical expenses amounts.

There is no provision for including the amount you have paid for drugs, in the medical expenses. The cause for not including them in the medical expenses is that they do not require any prescriptions. Thus, it would not be beneficial for you not to buy these drugs.

Finally, the result of Hypnosis on the smokers who wants to be a non-smoker is 70-80%. On the other hand, result of nicotine replacement pill is 50-60%. The cause of their low success rate is the inner consciousness of the user that, "I want to smoke and so I am substituting it." However, Hypnosis completely puts an end to smoker's inner consciousness and he never feels the desire to have it again.

CHAPTER 22- KILL YOUR ENEMY

People love chewing tobacco, although it is the source of several diseases. Being a harmful and toxic substance, tobacco is available everywhere. Moreover, there is no crime in selling this toxic substance, as it is legal to sell. Appropriate steps must be taken for banning this poison. It is like giving a license to kill.

Tobacco has harmed the humankind severely. Still no one is taking action against it. If the government helps in the fight of injustice or against terrorism or any natural or manmade calamity then why they are not paying concern to the tobacco. But, before reforming of the whole society, one should reform oneself.

Do not love your body?

You must know that smoking cigarette means giving entry to 4000 toxic chemicals into your body. You can imagine the amount of damage that these 4000 poisonous substances can do. Think for a while, of pouring adulterated fuel or any other harmful substances into your favorite car tank. You can easily estimate the damage you have done to your car. Similarly, making the entry of 4000 poisonous substances is like killing yourself.

Is it possible for you to pour harmful substances into your car?

No, you cannot do this to your car, then why you are doing this with you.

People are unable to quit smoke due to several of misconceptions. It is nothing but the addiction of nicotine that completely overpowers them.

For Instance, smokers say smoking makes them feel nice, or the taste of tobacco is simply great. There is one very common excuse for smoking is that to de-stress oneself. Whenever smoker gets tired, he felt the desperate need of cigarette.

All these are quite common excuses. Now, ask a non-smoker about these excuses of smoking. He would certainly be happy without smoking, as it makes him fit and healthy.

If you really want to quit smoking then simply decide not to smoke. Your own decision will help you in quitting smoking. Even a chain smoker can quit smoke if he determine firmly.

Just pay a serious concern to a few issues.

The first thing you must consider is your body; you must take care and keep it healthy.

Secondly, decision to kill your enemy who is killing you.

Thirdly, cost that smoking has caused for you. You have spent a lot on this poison. Lastly forget the past that will help you in quit smoking. Just remember that nicotine is my enemy and is killing me slowly.

Chapter 23- Lame Excuses Never Work

It is not easy for anyone to quit a habit quickly. One needs time and must be granted that duration to help oneself, but what about those who love to continue with this bad habit and even make excuses to retain it. It is common among chain smokers to search for lame excuses. One such excuse is 'Concentration Con'. A smoker explains that a puff helps him to concentrate. This excuse does not have any medical base but is just a fake explanation that renders a chance to the smoker to continue smoking.

Every habitual person who is in the process of getting rid of smoking has to face withdrawal symptoms but may not last long. At times, the person becomes irksome and restless. He takes this nature as a negative effect and again wants to have a puff to feel at ease. But when this misconception unveils itself, we come across a fact that smoking lessens the concentration power instead of enhancing it. The ease that the smoker feels after puffing another cigarette is just an effect of nicotine. Nicotine intoxicates the mind making it relax for a short time. This way the person feels temporary pleasure and takes smoking as his best buddy.

Nicotine works in a vicious circle. Its effect goes on increasing and after some time comes to the same point from where it has been started showing its black magic. Nicotine holds a smoker in such a way that he begins craving for more and more dose. If the smoker does not provide the requisite dose, he experiences restlessness. There is a vast difference between concentration power of a smoker and that of a non-smoker. It is an accepted fact that we derive less pleasure from the things that we always have. The same happens with a chain smoker. He goes on puffing and never reaches to a satisfaction level.

Doctors have concluded that cigarettes block arteries and reduce supply of oxygen to the brain due to which person lacks concentration. 'Concentration Con' is an outcome of psychological perceptions of most of the smokers. Those who use this excuse to shield their smoking need to be familiar with the underlying truth. Quitting the habit of smoking helps a person to take out his thinking man out of the smoke that has captured his mind. Veiling the smoking will not help. One needs to come forward to escape this habit rather than continuing it with the help of futile excuses.

CHAPTER 24- IT'S TIME TO THINK

Let's think in term of quitting smoking, although you are love with 'smoking'. You have to build up an honest sincere desire to give up smoking. Perhaps you have the felling how it is possible to quill smoking since you love so much to smoke.

Someone knowing fully well that if he drives his car in high speed may lead to an serious accident, still he does that. So it is like that you know smoking is bad for you but still you enjoy smoking.

You have to make up your mind to develop the desire to quit. You can now plan to draw up a list of merits of your smoking. You can also make a list of de-merits of smoking recently you experienced.

Be generous and make list of most idealistic reason that could lead you to quit smoking. You may like to prove yourself a great economist "save money for tomorrow", "be honest to your family", "The most obedient husband" etc.

Go on reading the lists every day. It will motivate you fast to quit smoking.

Fix an appointment with your physician to see a human lungs picture taken out of smoker's body. Ask your physician what good thing you are going to achieve after you have given up smoking etc.

When you have a definite desire to quit smoking you can really go through deeply with your list of 'benefits of smoking'. You may take a comparative statement how a non-smoker relives boredom while you cannot do without smoking what leads a non-smoker to relax and get away with stress etc.

You should be careful enough to know that much of the positive parts of smoking are temporary with no for reading results to yield good to you.

You have already examined your benefits you get while you smoke but now is the time to workout on replacement for your cigarettes by and by continue to receive benefits that smoking was providing you. Have a see through within yourself and find out is really the so called   benefits giving you any useful atmosphere where you can feel calm and relaxed. If so then try to consider the fact how a non-smoker relax.

So, in the list of your benefits add some more points which may replicate other than smoking. You can really feel different than what you are today; if you sincerely try re-invent your life.

CHAPTER 25- USEFUL TIPS TO GET RID OF SMOKING

1. Built up a strong belief in you blended with stronger will power to quit smoking. Consider giving up smoking as one of the very difficult things you have done in your life. It's all up to you.

2. Develop your plan and take a decision right away for doing things accordingly.

3. Make short note why you want to quit (benefits of quitting)live longer far better, for your family , some money, smell better to find a mate easily etc. you know very well what is bad about smoking and what you will achieve by quitting smoking. Put the same on a paper and read it daily once.

4. Seek an all-out support from your family and friends for your decision to quit. Tell them in the very near future you may become irritable, even irrational as a cause of quitting smoking habit.

5. Get on with a set date for quitting and also decide on what day you intend to say a final good-bye to cigarette. You may hold a small ceremony when you smoke your last cigarette. It's up to your liking.

6. Speak to your doctor about quitting. A whole hearted support from a physician would work out as proven way to better off your shames to quit.

7. An exercise program on daily basis is going to help you relive of stress, and recover from years of damage from cigarettes, may be you can start walking ones or twice per day. You may also consider about some rigorous activities 3 to 4 times per week. Consult your physician prior to begin any exercise program.

8. Practice some deep breathing every day 3 to 5 minutes breath in through the nose slowly hold breath for a few seconds, exhale slowly through your mouth.

9. Begin to visualize your way as a non-smoker. Close your eyes imagine yourself turning down offers of cigarettes, offered by someone, throwing all of your packs of cigarette away, winning a gold medal for doing so. A powerful visualization really works.

10. Cut back on cigarettes keep it with a gradual speed. (Make sure a quit date till then) This scenario would call for a clear cut plan as to 'how many cigarettes ' you will smoke everyday reducing the number following each day; you buy only one pack at a time, changing brands means you don't enjoy smoking as much pall on cigarettes to someone else when feel like to smoke you have to ask for each time.

11. Mostly smokers feel if to give up smoking take firm decision once for all, just to quit abruptly, no point trying to go slow and steady. You are the best judge quitting cold turkey or by gradual quitting.

12. Make a genuine attempt to find out another smoker who is also trying to quit help each other disusing some positive thought just because quitting becomes different.

13. You have 'clean sheet' now after quitting smoking your area nonsmoker. You can now think of celebrating the milestone of your journey step by step. After a period of two weeks see a movie, visit a funny restaurant a month after. Covering a time span of three months move out for you after six months. A year after have a party for yourself, invite your family friends to your birthday party, celebrate your new beginning of life.

14. To drink lot of water. Drinking of more would help flushing out nicotine and chemical out of your body.

15. Avoid triggers, learn to plan alternative means and way to deal with the trigger like you feel smoking when in stress, in the end of a meal, arrival at the work, entering a bar etc.

Chapter 26- Stop Smoking: Mission Impossible & Making It Possible

To leave one of your favorite habits is really a very tough thing. Even, cutting up the quantity is also a difficult thing to do. For Instance, after doing your check up, your doctor has advised you to take little amount of sugar in your tea or cut down the amount of salt in your food. Cutting the amount of either salt or sugar is very tough; you will feel as you are going through a torture. Similarly, if the lessening of amount is tough, then completely quitting up your favorite time pass or habit sounds impossible.

One will feel that he has been given a 'mission impossible' to accomplish. But, as we all know that smoking is like a poison and its only work is to destroy the person, who is having it with such a delight. The only thing one need is to determine to quit it at any cost. Do not bother about the time you are taking in quitting it. You have already taken the first step towards quitting this habit. If one even determines of quitting it, that means you have already won half of the battle.

It is quite possible that you will not get your desired destination in the very first attempt. So, never lost your cool, keep trying, and always remember that 'every cloud has a silver lining'.

To get rid of this smoking habit is a difficult task to perform, as cigarettes and all the smoking objects has nicotine in its content. Nicotine act as an addictive and the smoker becomes addicted to it. Nicotine enhances the quantity of dopamine in the body. When this dopamine enters the brain, the smoker gets a nice feeling, due to its effect.

Sometimes, experts advise to intake a little quantity of nicotine, until you get rid of it completely. It is a slow but in the meanwhile an effective process in getting rid of the smoking habit permanently. There are several products available in the market that can replace nicotine, such as nicotine patch or gum. Apart from all these options, the most important thing one must take care is the determination of quitting it permanently.

One major hindrance on your way to quit smoking is the routine you are following to smoke. In your daily routine, you have given a special place to this habit. While working in an office, you often smoke during intervals, or after dinner, or having drinks in a party, or when doing nothing, just to pass your time.

The first thing you must do is to decide a proper date that from this day onward 'quit smoking' mission starts. Begin this mission by not to smoke during these intervals. It may be possible in the beginning to find it a little difficult. So, try to divert your mind on some other things and slowly you will notice a considerable progress in you.

Your decision of getting rid of smoking completely is not only good for your health, but your family members will also get benefited from it. It will not only benefit your health wise but will also enable you to utilize these intervals creatively. Moreover, the money you were burning on it can also be used for some good cause.

While quitting this bad habit, do not get pessimistic but try to enjoy this phase with something constructive. The best thing one can do is to join any exercise program under the guidance of an expert trainer. Exercise is the proper replacement of smoking, as smoking makes you feel a little elevated, so do the exercise.

Always try to keep your hands and mouth busy by having chewing gum or ice cream or anything that engage your hands and mouth.

Quitting is not an easy task for the smoker. The smoker has to go through many difficult phases, but one should never dishearten and keep trying. One thing you must consider is to be ready for every kind of situations and still not giving up the determination.

The quitting of smoking will give you and your loved ones, lungs and hearts a new life.

Chapter 27- Stop Smoking: Your Determination Is Needed

Is it possible for a smoker to quit smoking?

It is quite tough for a smoker to leave his/her beloved. After all beloved is the one whom we cannot leave at any cost, at even our cost of life. But, do not you think that this beloved of yours is slowly but steadily destroying you. All the smokers are very well aware of all these things, but still they love to have it. The best way to put an end to this growing menace is by putting an end to its manufacturers.

Putting an end to its manufacturing is not possible, as the manufacturers are earning millions of dollars from these stupid smokers. We all know there will be no end of smokers until there are cigarettes available. In the same manner, as long as there are smokers, there are also the smokers who want to get rid of this bad habit. Interestingly, many counselors, doctors and companies are offering new ways of quitting this poison. Similarly, smokers are also of different varieties. If certain idea is effective on one smoker that does not mean this idea will work on the other smoker also. If such a thing happens then there will be no smoker in the world. There will be only one treatment that will be help the smoker in getting rid of it. The problem is that if something works for one smoker then it is not sure that it will also work for the other smoker. This is one of the main causes behind the ever-increasing smokers in the world.

Many researches on medicines that will be helpful in quit smoking by the major drug manufacturers, has not given the desired results. Millions of dollars have been spent on the invention of new medicines that will be helpful for smokers. However, this huge effort is only helpful for 20 to 50 percent of smokers. These drugs are quite fruitful in quitting smoking habits permanently, but as earlier said that there are different varieties of smokers. On some smokers these drugs works, but on others, they are simply useless.

After reading this, do not get disheartened. If someone is able to quit smoke with the drugs is fine. On the other hand, if you are unable to quit smoking then try some other way. There are millions of ways available, only thing that one needs, is the attitude or your determination. If your determination is strong and approaching with right attitude, then nothing in the world is impossible.

You are determined now that you are going to get rid of this bad habit. Now, nothing is impossible for you, as you have this much-needed will power and attitude. Go ahead, as there are many paths in front of you and there must be one path that will lead you to your destination. Therefore, the best way to quit smoking is the way that suits you. Your work is to keep trying until you succeed. Thus, never get disappointed that you are unable to quit smoking even after several attempts. Just tread along this path steadily and one day you will surely get rid of this bad habit. You must have heard, "Slow and steady wins the race".

CHAPTER 28- A PERSONAL ANALYSIS ON QUITTING SMOKE

It is a fact that smoking is more of psychological addiction than physical addiction. The Nicotine addiction in your body can be controlled, but mind addiction is tough to control.

One thing that helps you in quitting smoking is a complete personal analysis.

Take a paper and make two columns in it. In one column put heading, the cause for quitting. In another column, write down the cause for taking up smoking.

Firstly, write down the causes for taking up smoking. It may be some kind of pressure, or family trouble or financial trouble or any other reason. Now, find out whether these troubles still exist or not. If they do not, then there is no need to smoke.

Now, write down the causes for quitting smoking. It may due to the scare of deadly disease you may get, or your fear of passing them to your family members. Thus, health is one of the causes for quitting smoking.

However, it is quite possible that health reasons will not convince you in quitting smoking. They all have the possibilities. It is not sure that these things can happen. Lung cancer might happen or you may die early.

There are certain genuine causes that you are experiencing while smoking.

Write down those causes in the second column. For instance, you experience breathlessness while coming upstairs. Your feet are cold due to high blood pressure. You are always suffering from cough and it makes you feel uncomfortable.

Apart from health reasons, there are certain other reasons also. Such as, premature aging and drying of skin are due to smoking. Your fingernails, teeth are of yellow color and gives bad impression. When you smoke at public places, people make faces at you. You are spending a lot on cigarettes along with the mouth fresheners. You can save a huge amount by quitting smoking. You can use that amount for a good purpose. You can go for a holiday.

Think about your family. They would feel more secure, after your quitting smoking. Your house would be clean, no dirtier walls, or stinking cars. Several genuine reasons are there for quitting smoking.

Thus, you can divert your mind easily by thinking these genuine effects of smoking. However, your hands are still free. Try to make your hands busy by indulging it in some activities, for Instance knitting, cooking etc.

So, do not waste time and go ahead.

CHAPTER 29- USING THOUGHTS

We are well aware of the consequences of smoking. Still, we are unable to quit it. The cause for unable to quit smoking is the addiction of nicotine, along with the weak determination. A firm determination can make one able to leave this addiction of nicotine far behind. You only need to play certain mind games, as we all know that mind controls the body.

There are a few examples of mind games. For Instance, you have decided to quit smoke, but your decision is not firm. You have the habit to smoke with your friends. Before meeting them, your mind has already started working. You would find it tough to sit there without smoking. You would start feeling miserable and weak. You will become frustrate by these thoughts. Finally, you will start smoking. One can easily conclude that mind was the only thing that had prompted you in taking up smoking again.

On the contrary, you can avoid this situation. It only needs a little diversion of your mind. If you divert your mind on some other thing then surely you can help yourself. Along with the diversion, it need positive outlook on quitting smoking. Never feel that life will be miserable without smoking, or it is impossible to quit smoke.

Now, handle the same situation in this manner. You are going to meet your friends. Your mind will start working as usual. However, try to think positively. You should consider it big achievement, if you do not smoke with your friends. Never feel that life would be miserable, if you have not smoked. On the contrary, think that you are blessing a healthy life to you, as well as your family. You are able to breathe fresh air, after quitting smoking.

If you are unable to resist the temptation at your friend's place then do not go there. It would be better for you to avoid that place. Try to do something creative that will divert your mind completely.

Think about your kids. Take your family for a long drive. The quality time that you spent with them was more precious than wasting it by smoking with your friends. You will find that you were actually making yourself a fool by indulging in smoking activity.

Whenever your urge for smoke grows, only think about its bad effects upon you. The smoke has made you its slave. But, you have to overcome this slavery and quit smoking at any cost, as smoking is costing you a lot.

CHAPTER 30- READY, STEADY & GO

Half of your battle is over, once you have decided to quit smoking. However, after the decision of quitting smoking comes the much difficult part. The resisting of temptations and it also needs your determination. Whenever you feel the desire to smoke, just remember certain things and you can easily put an end to your temptations.

Suppose, your friends are smoking and inviting you to smoke then it would be better to leave the place. After leaving that place, remember these things.

The Cause of Your Quitting

Simply start thinking about the various reasons that lead you to quitting smoking. It would be more beneficial, if you carry a paper and list all the causes. Now, if you feel a craving for smoking then read the list of causes. After reading them, you will overcome over the temptation.

Always Be Ready

After quitting smoking, still you can meet temptation any time. It could be your friends or any particular place. So, you must be ready for such instances. In a blank paper, make two columns in it. On the first column, write the possible chances that can lead you to smoke, such as watching TV or drinking tea. On the second column, write the action that you will perform to divert the craving of smoking. For Instance, you can read a newspaper if you feel the craving for smoking. Try this formula and see it really works.

Water

If you are feeling a strong urge to smoke then chew something. Chewing will definitely consumes a lot of your time. After chewing, start drinking a glass of water with the help of straw. While doing this you will forget the desire to smoke. It would be beneficial if you drink 8 glasses of water.

Praise yourself

Whenever you pass a non-smoking week, do not forget to praise yourself. Always decide something in advance to gift yourself, after a non-smoking week. Write name of the gift on the paper, along with the non-smoking period. This will increase your spirit.

Divert Your Mind

You can divert yourself by doing any other task. Make a cup of tea or read a newspaper.

A Friend in Need is a Friend Indeed

Make a call to your close friend or anyone who can talk to you for a while. You will forget the craving for smoking while talking.

The Punch

Get a picture of smoker's lungs and always keep it with you. See the picture, when you feel the craving for smoking.

CHAPTER 31- SAY NO TO CIGARETTE

Smokers can give an endless list of excuses for smoking. Such as, some gets energy from smoking. Some look smart, when they smoke. Some are able to maintain their figure because of smoking. Some smokes, as they are lonely and sad. Some smoke to celebrate. This list of excuses never ends. There are some exceptional cases also. Such as, a woman was suffering from chest pain after quitting smoking. The chest pain was cured when she started smoking again.

However, none of the given excuses is logical. There is only one reason for smoking. It is the addiction. The addiction is more psychological than physical. Smokers are actually addicted to those toxic chemical substances.

Nicotine is one of the major components of addiction in Cigarette smoking. The smoker is unable to get rid of this nicotine. The Nicotine is running in his blood level. When the level of Nicotine decreases in the blood, he shows certain nicotine withdrawal symptoms. The smoker smokes to cover up the deficiency of Nicotine in the blood level.

This nicotine withdrawal symptom clearly shows the cause for smoking relieving the stress. Some physiological effects also occur due to stress, such as, the urine acidic.

Smoking helps in calming them down is a general misconception. It does not reduce their stress. On the contrary, it maintains the reducing level of nicotine in blood that make them relieved.

Similarly, consumption of Alcohol also enhances the level of smoking. The Nicotine level drops and to compensate the dropping level smoker smokes a lot while drinking. Thus, it is important for the smoker to know the real cause for their smoking. It is not calming down their stress, but to maintain the level of poison in their body. This thought will help the smoker to be an ex-smoker.

Once you have decided to quit smoking from that very day this poison will start reducing in your body. Make a promise not to touch it again. Within two weeks, this poisonous substance nicotine will leave your body. You will experience no nicotine withdrawal symptoms and would be able to live normally.

You will realize the benefits of quitting smoking, only after quitting it. All the advantages of smoking were nothing but misconceptions. You will get an independent feeling within you. Now, you are no longer addict of anything.

However, the ex-smokers have to take extra care. The moment they chew tobacco or taken a single puff, you will become nicotine addict again. So, keep distance from cigarette.

CHAPTER 32- SMOKERS & EX-SMOKERS

Smokers always feel that smoking helps them in getting rid from unhappiness, stress, boredom, anxiousness and loneliness. The life without a cigarette means complete boredom and frustration. Most of the smokers feel that they will put on weight after quitting cigarette. They can work faster and better after a puff of cigarette. While smoking they can be more sociable. Smoking is also a way to celebrate on special occasions. Smokers feel that everything loses its charm without smoking. They are unable to enjoy social gathering, fun, games, drink, or even the company of their spouse. According to this data of smokers, smoking has so many great attributes.

However, one more data contradicts this data. In America, almost 33, 000, 000 Americans have quitted smoking and are leading a healthy life. A non-smoker would never be able to understand the great qualities of cigarette. However, the ex-smokers are well aware of these wonderful qualities. Still they have decided to quit. Are these 33, 000, 000 people mad?

These people are not mad, but they understood the disadvantages of smoking. They had also gone through the painful withdrawal symptoms of Nicotine. Still, they managed all the pain. They fought not only with the physical addiction, but also with the psychological addiction. The psychological addiction is a little tough, but they managed that too. They convinced themselves fully about the bad consequences of smoking. This demands a lot of firm determination from their side and a positive approach.

These smokers must be appreciated for coming out from this addiction. The earlier phase of quitting makes smoker a little insecure. However, you must have confidence on yourself that it is possible to live without cigarettes.

Once come out of the tight and dangerous grip of smoking. You will understand that you were on a wrong track. You were living in the world of misconceptions. After quitting smoking, they will realize that life without smoking is healthier, calmer and beautiful.

It depends on the ex-smoker, whether he/she wants to smoke again or not. Now, it demands a logical reasoning from you. However, many smokers again start smoking. The cause for their again taking up smoking is that they forgot the bad consequences of smoking. There is one more cause of taking up smoking again is the urge that they are unable to resist.

Therefore, all ex-smokers have two choices, either to quit it or to start smoking again. It is useless to be an occasional smoker, as it is also harming you a lot. Thus, make a promise of not letting even a little bit of Nicotine into your body.

CHAPTER 33- SMOKING: AN ADDICTION OR PHOBIA

Smoking a much better talked about issue presently, is fast becoming an addiction with smokers. Perhaps you never have thought on those lines simply because you felt that smoking is an important part of your life style.

You may not remember when started smoking; may be when you were very young or you were thrilled when you saw your friends smoking. After a short period you may have had the feeling that you could not do with smoking, which must have had created tension with you.

Later on, you may have felt whatever your parents try to make you understand about the ill effects of smoking on your health was right. You must have tried to get rid of smoking but then you may have been unable to take a decision as to what may happen to your smoking breaks.

The facts findings show differences about smoking as an addition with every smoker. A smoker would term smoking as a 'stimulant' or smoking which may provide him extra energy or so. The smoker is totally unaware that the stimulant is simply an addiction which is constantly completing him to remain hooked and not allowing him to come out of it.

Adopt a positive attitude, uncovering your self about smoking, its negative and positive effects on you as you feel. Now if really care to take a close look at what happens to you when you don't smoke or don't get cigarettes. You may feel lonely, bored; you may feel irregularly; you feel you need to touched up with glow when you light up a cigarette, so on and so forth. The non-smokers on the other hand relax on their own naturally, they don't require a light up cigarette to relax. You may go through some simple steps below to know about what you are addicted to and how to combat it.

- For a day or two whenever you smoke you write down the feelings you had before smoking every cigarette. Not whether felt bored, tired, and hungry, exhausted, or stress out.
- Write down some 'plus' points you experienced after smoking that cigarette, you may have felt sleepy, it may have helped you to make up early or reduced your boredom.
- If you review your list, you may find a pattern to your addiction.
- A total diversion of your thoughts, surely help you distract your feeling of smoking.
- It's not that difficult to give up smoking if you are sincere about it.

CHAPTER 34- SMOKING: MAKING A FOOL OF YOURSELF

Whenever you talk with a smoker and advise him/her to quit smoking, he/she will give thousands of reasons of unable to quit smoking. For Instance, they consider smoking as a thing that helps in de-stressing from anxiety. On the other hand, it is impossible for them to resist the temptation of smoking. They had included smoking in their daily routine. They are completely addicted to it.

Nicotine is the substance of addiction. Experts consider nicotine as the most addictive substance. In spite of this, they are unable to prove that nicotine can lead to physical addiction. Nicotine does not lead to high physical addiction.

There are certain substances such as Heroin, Cocaine that are highly addictive. When addicts do not get the doses of Heroin and Cocaine, they becomes out of control. They are unable to manage themselves without the intake of these substances. On the other hand, if a smoker quits smoking then nothing happens like this. Their bodies are in complete control. Several of smokers quit smoking daily but they never experience any physical problems.

Even chain smokers never smoke by waking up at night. But, a Heroin or Cocaine addict often wakes up at night to have it. They are able to sleep only after having it.

While watching a movie in a theater a smoker can simply spend a couple of hours without having a cigarette. This shows clearly that smoking is not at all a physical addiction. But, there are smokers who claim that they cannot sit for such long hours without cigarette. Thus, we can only say 'Exceptions are always there'.

Now, one can easily conclude that cigarette smoking is simply not addictive. If it leads to certain addiction then you cannot live without it for long hours. Like in several flights, smoking is prohibited or in various public places, you cannot smoke.

You are making yourself fool by assuring yourself that smoking is an addiction. Thus, you are unable to quit it. Smoking Cigarette means killing yourself by inviting several dreadful diseases. Smoking can only harm you, whether physically or financially.

The ever-growing Tobacco companies are the one, gaining from your smoking. They are only making you fool by selling this poison to you. Along with these companies, you are also making a fool of yourself. Before quitting smoking, smokers already declare that they could not live without smoking.

Now whenever you decide to quit then remind yourself only one thing. That quitting smoking will not lead to any physical problems and it is not a physical addiction.

CHAPTER 35- SMOKING: A NEVER ENDING PROBLEM

In spite of so much awareness about the ill effects of nicotine, smoking apparently continues to chase everyone, everywhere. It not only influences our lifestyle but also affects the lifestyle of our colleagues and family members. They too may become part of this habit or psychological concerns that may result from this addiction.

Earlier, smoking was a craze among adults only but now teenagers too have joined the trend. A surprising fact is that adults are more likely to quit smoking on being encouraged by friends, family and counselors, but getting teenagers to quit smoking is not all that easy. They start smoking under the influence of the peer group or friends, and even if they try getting out of the addiction, the same influences do not allow that to happen. Teenagers get well entrapped wherefrom it is not that easy to escape.

Smoking is making its presence felt in every sphere of our life, be it a school, home or work area. It is more an addiction than habit and therefore no one is able to escape its clutches in the first go.

Smoking is not only injurious to health but to one's wallet as well. Studies showing expenditure made on the pack of cigarettes has come with stunning outcomes. A person could have easily afforded a comfortable life with the money that one wastes on buying these stuffs. But the thing is that we never think about such consequences that are adversely affecting our life to a great extent.

In USA, it has been made mandatory for employees not to smoke at work. In case someone does not follow the rule, the Company has a right to fire that employee. Such smokers will not be insured by the Company. This has become a hot topic on the chat shows in America.

Most of the smokers are working hard to quit the habit of smoking but unfortunately, a few of them are able to do it. Many counselors have developed a program that has been proved successful for interested volunteers. This 'stop smoking' program works according to the Behavior Theory. It is different from other programs and helps a person not to depend on cigarettes at every tense circumstance of his life. This way the smoker learns to resist his cravings for another puff.

It has become essential to take necessary steps to control smoking before we have any more sufferers in its grasp. Friends, family and counselors can only suggest but one has to take the initiative on one's own to enter a healthy lifestyle.

CHAPTER 36- SMOKING: A NURTURER OR DESTROYER

Smokers are generally very eager as well as anxious to quit smoking. Smoking has leaded them at the threshold of many diseases like heart attacks, cancers, emphysema. Most of the smokers know that smoking is rotting their body from inside and slowly have started deteroiting their physical charm. Still smoking is their buddy and still an existing problem. We need to search for the reason of its existence.

Many smokers associate several activities with their smoking. The lure of continuing those activities persuades them to endure smoking as well. These activities include their daily routine. For them, being a non-smoker means that life has lost its importance. Smokers also think that he has to come across painful symptoms while working for quitting smoking. These reasons keep a smoker away from taking up of good habits. They can die from smoking but are afraid to quit.

If every one of us starts following thinking of the above sited smokers, then life will certainly lose its significance without smoking. But the fact is that they all are living under misconceptions. They will live a better life after quitting smoking than living with smoking. Pleasure that a smoker gets after the puffs is a deceptive pleasure and just the effect of nicotine that blocks our thinking power. Convincing smokers about this sometimes become next to impossible. These pleasures work as a stopper for smokers.

When smokers get out of their bed they feel slight headache, depressed that arouses a need for a cigarette in them and they go for it. When he feels depressed then also he feels for a cigarette or two to relax his nerves. Therefore he begins to expand his friendship with this deadly drug. But these are the symptoms that are taking them to their destruction.

If a smoker starts giving some space for the realities then he can quit smoking. He himself will be surprised to see the changes. He will feel taking up the things more efficiently than before. Morning will bring a different freshness for him. Feeling of panic reactions under the stress that were the outcome of the lower level of the nicotine will not be scaring him anymore. And slowly he will see the true face of smoking that once was his best buddy. Any ex-smoker can experience his growing strength, increased energy level than before when he was a smoker.

Even his fear of withdrawal symptoms will not last for many days. They would peak within three days and will completely lose their existence in all more two weeks. He will experience a simpler, happier, cleaner and above all a healthy life ahead of him.

CHAPTER 37- SMOKING & CONNECTED DISEASES

A research review reveals smoking and weight loss can never go together. The most talked over issue of the day is obese population. The health care people are trying to find out useful alternatives, towards obese along with important community. A number of options have already come up to cope up obese, as fast as possible.

Some of concrete truth about smoking and its co-related solution to the problem of excess of body weight; have look over myths and reality about smoking in the next paragraph.

A statistical observation by US centers for disease control and prevention points out that women are quitting smoking more in numbers than that of men. Data connected by the centers put down the percentage of women smokers to 20%even below than that in 2003 the figures of women smokers was only 19.2% compared to male smokers at 24.1%.

The opinion holds that exposure to cigarette smoking may cause damage to woman fertility. A study compiled about embryo quality and fertilization, divided into three groups. Says there was clear evidence of differences in the pregnancy rates per embryo transfer, it is around 48% with non-smokers, the smokers around 19% and with the others 20%.

Smoking and impotence have practically no relationship. As of now it has been found that cigarette smoking invites innumerable deadly disease like lung cancer, heart disease emphysema, erectile dysfunction etc. the ill effects of smoking can affect the digestive system and may be the cause of human importance.

To generalize the facts quitting smoking will not lesson the importance. Men who have erection problem may try to create some improvement by quitting smoking.

But according to doctors once the spot is damaged it cannot be restored by quitting smoking. Since everybody is different it may improve or even may not improve. The whole world knows about Viagra for erection. For some owe it may not work, especially to heart patients Viagra strictly forbidden.

Quitting smoking is possible if you ready think on in twice looking at the reason below.

- The factors that involve cancer risk.
- Money
- Bad breath
- Stained teeth and fingers
- Cough sore throat.
- Breathing problem
- Fatigue
- Wrinkles
- Arguments with friends or
- Spouse who wants you to stop smoking
- Heart disease risk
- Gum disease etc.

Think if you are following a right pain.

CHAPTER 38- SMOKING & PREGNANCY

Smoking, as such, is considered harmful for health. But, pregnancy is a state where one has to be very particular about certain habits, including smoking. You might have your reasons to smoke, but not at the cost of your health, and not at all at your baby's expense. Who would not love to have a healthy baby? May be, smoking would-be mothers do not, or do they! If you are planning to have a baby, quit the habit of smoking first. Do not play around with your and your child's health.

You may have a look into the effects of smoking on pregnant mothers. Nicotine and carbon monoxide are poisonous substances that can cause a lot of harm inside the body. During pregnancy, smoking leads to increase in the levels of carbon monoxide and nicotine in the mother's bloodstream. These substances have frightening effects on the mother's body, as the blood vessels are constricted and restricted, effecting the supply of oxygen and nutrients. The baby is denied its full share of nutrients and oxygen, which hampers the growth of the baby. You can compare the whole scenario to your being hungry and being offered an insufficient amount of food laced with poisonous substances. When you smoke, this is what exactly your baby experiences.

Babies born to mothers who smoke during pregnancy are likely to be premature. If the pregnancy lasts a full term, the baby may be born underweight and small. Such babies need special care under medical supervision, which extends their stay in hospital.

During pregnancy, the baby of a smoking mother is denied proper oxygen, which can lead to miscarriages or fetal brain damage. Sudden infant death syndrome can be a result of smoking, according to certain studies. Smoking is found to affect the blood pressure of the developing baby. This adversely affects its development and the child's learning ability, like attention deficit disorder retarded mental growth. The child may also develop respiratory problems like asthma, when young.

Once your baby is born, it still is needed to be protected from smoking. Smoking leads to reduction in milk supply, and can hamper breastfeeding. Moreover, the baby gets a fair dose of nicotine through breast milk, which can cause illness in the form of diarrhea, nausea, colic etc. Second hand smoke is not good for the baby, since it affects the lungs through the nicotine it inhales. You would not like your baby to develop breathing problems.

Chapter 39- Smoking Has Tendency To Affect Your Spirits

People have their own reasons to smoke.

Some people smoke to relax and some to feel more alert when they feel dull. Some take up smoking because they want to relax their nerves when feel stressed, bored or to overcome their anger. A cigarette becomes their doctor, their buddy, their life. It all happens because of chemicals present in cigarettes. These chemicals result in psychological effects that they have on the nerves of a smoker.

The head of these chemicals is Nicotine. It works as a stimulant. It has the same components and functions that cocaine, amphetamine has. Smokers want to have a boost up feeling when they feel depressed, irritated and frustrated. The resistance to overcome all these feelings is provided by the nicotine. It also increases their heart rate, blood pressure and breathing rate due to which a smoker feels more alert than before. It helps in his spontaneous but deceptive recovery. After sometime a smoker finds himself at the same point with more deteriorating health. Cigarette has products like acetaldehyde and carbon monoxide. Carbon monoxide is harmful of all the substances. It makes one feel dull as if someone has locked you in the stuffy room. These chemicals have property of reducing the tensions, anger and irritation. They hold these feelings but not eliminate them. Something which is suppressed comes out more strongly. This same case happens in smoking.

People smoke, when taking coffee, consuming alcohol and eating desserts. It becomes a comfortable habit for them and they start taking it for granted. A smoker gets involved in different fantasies as he feels that his stress is bothering him less after a puff, he is able to concentrate more.

Getting addicted

Initially a smoker smokes for false pleasure but when he continues his habit, he does so out of his habit for having nicotine. Until and unless he gets a dose of nicotine, he cannot work properly. He gets addicted to the deadly drug.

Need to understand

Try to differentiate between feelings when you were craving for the puff and when you have finished with your cigarette. The come up differences will make you understand your position that later will help you to quit the smoking.

CHAPTER 40- SMOKING: MORE A HABIT, LESS A PLEASURE

Smokers failed to experience desired pleasure from smoking. To get their intended bliss, they keep on switching from one product to another when they feel that their brand is not gratifying them anymore. Initially when smoker begins smoking, he experiences warmth that seems him to fill their hollowness. Therefore they take this deadly drug as their life long companion. This delight that they enjoy is nothing but a pharmacological action of nicotine. It relaxes the smoker nerves depriving him of his thinking power. Smoking gives him false impression of being confidant, mature, and more social.

We all want to escape the bad circumstance of our life. Similarly when a smoker wants to do the same, smoking lends him a helping hand and gives all the false happiness to him that he has always wanted. This forces him to puff more like 5 to 6 cigarettes a day. But gradually he gets dependent on the cigarettes. Then his habit urges him to puff more not his problem. If he does not answer his urge then he feels irritated, frustrated, nervous, angry, and nauseous and ignored. To ease these symptoms he has to smoke and all the time he hopes that he will get support from the cigarettes and that becomes dream for him. He does feel better but only for a little time and after that blessed minutes the process again shape up itself.

The effects after quitting smoking bless him. He does not experience those horrible urges, headaches and no longer does he get into those withdrawal symptoms. He begins enjoying his liberty without worrying all time about need of smoking. His headache also gives him the pleasure because now he knows that this headache is a part of the process that ensures his healthy lifestyle.

But again something happens inside him. He starts re-picturing the warmth given by his best cigarette in his life. Long thinking about it forces him to focus on it and to bring that same pleasure in his life again that he obeys. Once again he got caught up in the same grip of an addiction. In this grip he smokes more and enjoys it less. He wants to continue to survive in the same grip at the cost of his liberty, his health and is life. Smokers who really want to enjoy their life with its true meaning needs to concentrate on the side effects of smoking otherwise they will find themselves at the threshold of the death.

Chapter 41- Smoking: Not A Solution

Stress is directly proportional to smoking. All the smokers out there will agree with this fact. It is a common slogan of all the smokers that because they smoke of stress. But, this is a misconception. People often get stressed, due to their smoking habit. Even after quitting smoking, smokers often start smoking. The main causes for taking up smoking again are social gatherings, parties, stress and alcohol.

There are several smokers, who want to get rid of this deadly chemical. After few failed attempts, they even say bye to smoking. But, after a certain period their urge for smoking begins. They feel that life is boring without smoking. The ex-smoker becomes nervous, upset and depress without smoking. These kinds of depressions are one of the effects of not smoking.

In our daily life, we experience stress everywhere. The stress can be job related or family or friends or financial. In such stressful situations, the ex-smoker wants to take the help of smoking. He would go for smoking, as he thinks it to be helpful. However, this is a complete misconception of him.

For Instance, you are having a lot of work pressure in the office. If you use to smoke earlier, then you would immediately think of having cigarette.

Is it reasonable of having cigarette in such a situation?

Instead of organizing the schedule of your work, you are thinking about having cigarette. Can you give any cause for having cigarette in this situation? Neither cigarette can help you in easing the work pressure, nor can do the work. Thus, there is no cause for smoking in such stressful situation. You are only making a fool of yourself.

You are again allowing the entry of numerous deadly chemicals. These chemicals will result in harmful deadly diseases. Moreover, your near and dear ones are also being affected.

Thus, the job stress is nothing in front of these deadly diseases. The smoking will make you more anxious. It enhances the frustration. You will take another cigarette, when the first one ends. In this way, you will start smoking again. You have quitted smoking, after several failed and sincere attempts. But, due to certain stress you are again taking it up. Even, if you are going through some major crisis period, remember that smoking will not get the solution for you. Several times, we are unable to handle our situations. Such as, death of a near one or getting bankrupt, or major illness and ended up in taking cigarette. But, always remember that smoking is not going to solve your problem.

CHAPTER 42- SMOKING: THE GAME OF NICOTINE

Everyone is well aware of the bad consequences of smoking, even the smokers. Still, they do not quit smoking. One major cause for their not quitting smoking is their love for smoking. Most of the smokers would agree to this fact that they love smoking. But, do not you think it is a wrong word for smoking. It is actually a misconception. The cause for their smoking do not depends on their love for smoking. But, the real cause is that they do not like not smoking.

Several deadly chemicals enter through smoking. Nicotine is one of the major content of cigarette. It is an addiction, making the smoker addicted for it. This Nicotine is running along the blood stream of smoker. When the level of Nicotine decreases in the smoker's blood level, he/she will become tense. The smoker needs continuous doses of nicotine in his/her blood to behave normally. When the level of nicotine decreases, the smoker would immediately smoke. After smoking, the level of nicotine becomes normal and smoker would be automatically normal. This is the only cause for smoking.

Nicotine should be consumed up to a limit. The exceeding limit of nicotine content in your body can do serious harm to your body. A successful smoker is the one, who is able to manage the content of nicotine.

When smokers decide to quit, they have to gone through several difficult phases.

They are well aware of the pain that they are going to experience without smoking. The earlier phases are very tough, as they have to face the problem due to decreasing nicotine level. The urge for smoking will be too strong. But, gradually their urge slows down.

Smoker has the tendency to smoke frequently. However, when the interval grows, they will be able to manage themselves without smoking. In this way, one can quit smoke.

But, if you continue smoking no one can help you. You need your help in quitting smoking. Otherwise, ruin your life in your continuous battle for maintaining the level of nicotine. This harmful fight costs your life as well as your bank balance. You have already wasted a huge amount in buying this poison. Along with the money, you are also destroying your precious health.

Only one puff of smoke causes the entry of so many deadly chemicals in your body. Next time when your urge for smoke arises, just remember these words.

CHAPTER 43- THE ART OF QUITTING SMOKING

Quitting smoking does not make everyone gain weight but it results in gaining a few extra pounds. Weight gain is much possible for chain smokers. It gives the smoker the false feeling of weight gain which is actually due to water retention after which the body comes to its previous position.

Chain smokers are more prone to health dangers when they try to quit smoking and the main symptom is weight gain.

How to preserve health after quitting smoking:

1. Physical fitness

➢ Daily exercise can be a good reminder to make one realize that how much of the energy he has lost due to smoking as he will find it quite tough to exercise properly. Physical fitness enhances your energy levels and by bringing you close to the nature, it also diverts your mind off smoking.
➢ Beginners should exercise for 30 minutes initially not essentially on regular basis. Exercise not only ensures good health but also helps in controlling weight. You can go for exercises like brisk walking and playing.

2. Good eating habits

➢ Good eating habits ensure prevention of weight gain and make you feel good. Eating nutritious diet on regular basis helps a lot but you should not change yourself too fast as it can result in fatigue.
➢ Never try to quit smoking during bouts of tension only to prevent snacking. It can result in consuming more snacks or

taking to smoking again and the person becomes addicted once again.

3. Resisting longings

➢ Once you quit smoking, you should also learn how to resist craving for cigarettes and food. If one learns to overcome craving for 5 minutes, then it generally goes off.
➢ Try to busy your hands and mouth with things like chewing gum, solving puzzles to replace smoking.
➢ Try not to accompany your loneliness with tea or coffee. It can increase the nervous feeling.
➢ Have required sleep when tired and also try to lessen your anger and loneliness. Go for meditation and relax properly.
➢ Take up another subject to talk other than smoking.
➢ List the places where you feel urge to smoke and also list things you can have as a substitute of smoking. Avoid going to the pubs, having chips when watching television.
➢ Some anxious smokers can also go for nicotine gum or patch known for reducing the weight gain only on being prescribed by the doctor.

4. Be optimistic

➢ Eating habits become better with the passage of time as you left smoking and food tastes nice when you become habitual of eating healthy food.
➢ Don't be pessimist and let yourself not to be afraid about weight gain. If it happens you will surely lose weight with the help of your eating habits and be confident about your choice to stay healthy.

CHAPTER 44- THE DEADLY SECONDHAND SMOKE

When a person inhales smoke that comes out from the burning of tobacco is known as side stream smoke. On the other hand, when a person inhales smoke while a person is smoking is called the mainstream smoke. Both these types of smoking are called Secondhand smoke or ETS.

Do you know the number of poisonous substances we inhales while a person smokes?

The ETS mainly consist of about 4000 poisonous substances. They make entry into our body and 40 among them can be carcinogens. Whether you are smoking or just inhaling the smoke exhaled by a smoker, it does not matter. The consequences are dangerous and lead to several respiratory problems.

ETS belongs to the class of carcinogens. The amount of carcinogen in ETS is much higher. The cause for high rate of carcinogen in ETS is that it is unfiltered. Thus, active smoker is inhaling lower quantity of carcinogen than the ETS.

There are two main places in cigarette that produces smoke. The tip of the cigarette is the one from where smoke released. Secondly, the hot smoke releases through the cigarette and its filter from the remaining part of the cigarette.

The major portion of ETS incorporates cigarette's burning tip. It is around 70 to 80 percent of ETS. The major components are nicotine, tar, carbon monoxide and carcinogens. Thus, ETS is more harmful and deadly than the person smoking directly.

There are several hazards of Secondhand smoke. It causes eye irritation, sore throat, dizziness, nausea, headache and cough.

Apart from these effects, it also leads to certain long-term illness. The major disease caused by it is the lung cancer. When a non-smoker suffers from a deadly disease like lung cancer it is because of Secondhand.

Based on recent survey, it is found that hospitality workers have more chances of lung cancer. Those workers who are more exposed to secondhand smoke have more chances of acquiring this deadly disease.

Cardio vascular problems are also one of the diseases caused by the secondhand smoke. Certain chemicals block arteries and that leads to heart attack or hypertension. Asthma and Breast cancer are also caused by secondhand smoke.

Your children are also getting affected and have more chances of acquiring deadly diseases.

If a pregnant woman smokes then she is harming her baby directly. The baby will be of low-weight; size of lungs will be smaller and have more chances of tobacco addiction.

CHAPTER 45- THE PSYCHOLOGICAL THERAPY

Addiction of smoking is actually the addiction of nicotine. Nicotine is the one that causes addiction and makes difficult for people to quit smoking. There are several nicotine replacement gum or patches are available in the market. Do you think it to be reasonable of quitting smoking with the help of another nicotine product?

Our main concern is getting rid of nicotine and clearing our body from the nicotine. Making the body completely free from nicotine is our real job. But, we are making another way for nicotine in our body. Nicotine is the main cause for all cravings and temptations. The first thing we must do is to throw nicotine out from the body. Its exit is the only way to quit smoking.

Secondly, nicotine gives calmness or de-stress our anxiety. It gives us light feeling or generate nice feeling into us. So, we must look for a replacement at time of anxiety. Try to divert your mind in something else, such as drinking water, exercising, making a phone call or preparing a cup of tea.

Lastly, you need to take care of this old habit. There must be certain places or people, where you enjoying your smoking. Try to avoid this by doing something more creative.

Smoking becomes the habit of smoker. It is a well-known fact that habits are hard to leave. Thus, it obvious that smoker has to face a lot of problem while quitting smoking. But, he should determine firmly to quit smoking. Always remember the bad effects of nicotine in your body and your determination of getting rid from it.

Do not let your senses overpower you.

Aromatherapy oil blend will be helpful in getting rid of the habits that leads to smoking. Follow these steps and see it will work.

The first thing you should do is to keep this oil near the cigarettes of smoker.

Then try to place this oil near the lip like a cigarette. Take a couple of deep breaths, so that the aroma should be inhaled.

This is like a trick your brain in forgetting the addiction of nicotine. This act is quite similar to smoking; here you are also inhaling something. Aromatherapy will be helpful in forgetting the nicotine habit and will act as its substitute. You can also call it as a psychological phenomenon. If the smoker is able to resist the craving for two minutes then surely he can quit smoking.

CHAPTER 46- THINK ABOUT IT

Smokers who are smoking from long time become habitual to smoking. They do not find any harm in smoking. They have included smoking as their daily routine. Many smokers often decide to quit smoking. On the other hand, several smokers do not find any benefits in quitting smoking. They feel that smoking helps them a lot. For Instance, smoking relieves them from anxiety and makes them feel light. They would not be able to work properly without smoking. Thus, they do not find much benefit in quitting smoking.

But, they are not aware what they are missing.

The benefits of quitting smoking are so vast that they cannot even imagine. The major benefit is health. They will be able to lead a healthy and active life, after quitting smoking.

Once you quit smoke the risk of heart disease gradually decreases up to half within a year. After 15 years of non-smoking, your risk of heart disease would be almost equivalent to a non-smoker. Thus, your heart will be as normal as of non-smoker.

Quitting also decreases the dangers of lung cancer. The danger of lung cancer decreases up to 30 to 50 percent, after ten years. If your age is 35 then after quitting smoking, you are giving 7 to 8 more years to you. If a woman quits at the age of 35 then she is incrementing her life from 6 to 8 years. You can add 6 to 7 more years to your life, if you are at the age group of 45. 3 to 6 years can be added, if you are 55. Moreover, 1 to 1.4 if you are 65.

Thus, you can always enjoy the benefits of healthy life and clean environment around you. It only depends on you. What you want from your life?

Would you like to have deadly diseases or want to lead a healthy life?

Choice is yours. You can opt for life and at the same time death also.

Your time span of smoking does not matter at all. The thing that really matters is enjoying the benefit of quitting smoking. When quitting smoking guarantees so many advantages then one should quit smoke without giving a second thought.

Do not play with your life. Life is precious. Your smoking habit is slowly, but steadily killing you. Moreover, you are playing on your money. Smoking has only disadvantages.

Why do not you quit it?

Think about it.

Chapter 47- Tips To Control Smoking

There are different ways which enables a person to control smoking as well as weight:

- Tickle yourself with a comedy recording or a comedy video.
- Do not fix to daily routine and same dress. Change it time to time.
- Listen to cassettes regarding fatigue control.
- Try to tighten all body parts and then relax.
- Add brisk waking, cycling, deep breathing and swimming in your exercise.
- Enroll yourself in gym.
- Take a balanced diet consist of salad, green leafy vegetables and pulses.
- Less salt, sugar, fat containing diet and visit dietician time to time.
- Enjoy yourself with classical music and nature sound recordings.
- Close your eyes and slowly focus your mind on one word which makes you stress free.
- Try to talk on subject other than smoking, enjoy yourself in others company.
- Take time to go out on long vacation to hill stations.
- Take drive to peaceful places like meadow, beach, and forests.
- Be optimist and try to escape aggression. Go for courses like sailing, painting, yoga.
- Lend hand to needy person and involve with new activities whether social or cultural.
- Make new friends and be thankful to your blessings.
- Have a warm bath with good bath oils like lavender.

- Fancy yourself at an acquainted peaceful place and then try to relax your body parts one by one. The art is known as self-hypnosis.
- Some hospitals conduct stress reduction classes. Call to get timings about next sessions.
- Everyone cannot be right at every time so do not bother yourself over one subject. Choice is always available to everyone.
- Set your exercise and relaxation schedule. Overdrinking of coffee can be dangerous.
- Be thankful to all your comforts, friends, family and above all your work.
- List your work according to priorities and tackle them with care giving top priority to your personal life and family.
- If a task is bothering you, divide it into mall tasks.
- Your energy is precious so do not waste it on less important task.
- Appreciate your subordinates and take pleasure in getting compliments.
- Adopt 'never to say die' attitude.
- Nurture hopes and goals within yourself.
- Get involve in things which give you feeling of relaxation and happiness. Let your inner self not to get heavy on you.

Above mention tips will certainly ensure your happy and healthy stay.

CHAPTER 48- TOBACCO: NOT A CONSUMER PRODUCT

Tobacco addiction is one of the worst addictions, with the number of tobacco users and smokers having crossed the one billion-mark worldwide. What is a cause for concern is that smoking has been and is being marketed as a fashionable product; a product that is projected to be responsible for the death of over half a million smokers this year.

Tobacco is being promoted and projected as a consumer product. Not being aware of the harmful effects of tobacco, the young generation is sucked into believing that it is fashionable to smoke. At an influential age, the youngsters lap up every advertisement targeted at them and take to smoking without realizing the ill effects waiting to consume them. For that matter, you may call tobacco a "consumer product", because it "consumes" your health and even your life, if you are not that lucky.

It is unbelievable that such a harmful product that causes addiction, sickness and even painful death, is allowed to be marketed freely. Tobacco is among the few anti-health products that are legally allowed to be sold as consumer products. Such is the impact of the bombardment of cigarette smoking advertisements that the warning label on every cigarette pack is overlooked. It is the 'it-can-never-happen-to-me' attitude coupled with glamour attached to smoking, which is the undoing of most smokers.

Smoking is a serious addiction and every addict needs help urgently to get out of the habit. Tobacco reform laws need to be strict, in addition to heavy imposition of taxes, which can discourage people from getting addicted. The idea is to make the availability of tobacco and nicotine difficult. People may argue that despite the ban on drugs, and their availability at prohibitive prices drug trade continues to flourish. The counter to such arguments is what could have been the situation today had the consumption of drugs not been illegalized. We may have had to confront a situation where every household had a drug addict or two.

Imposing a sudden ban on smoking or use of nicotine is not a very practical solution. This will leave the addicts high and dry. The entire process has to be a well thought out exercise. Educational programs on the ill effects of smoking need be developed, along with all possible professional and emotional help to help people get out the addiction. This is going to be a massive common exercise involving the state, the corporate world, and of course, the common man.

CHAPTER 49- WANT TO QUIT SMOKING?

Quitting the smoking is a desire that chain smokers wish to come true. It can be possible with the following:

Have confidence: If you can believe yourself then you have already won half of the battle. Try to re- picture your days when you have proved your willpower. The only thing that you need is to boost up your spirits again.

Try with the limitations of smoking first. Think how smoking is eating up your body and then go for the advantages. Start applying them on yourself as quitting smoking will increase you lifespan, will make you feel better.

Family is precious for all. Think how much you will save if you quit smoking. It will help you in making new friends who hates smoking and will help you to do the same.

Initially you will behave illogically means that you will be restless. At that time remember your friends and family is there to help you out .Ask them to be tolerant with you and support you.

Exercise will allow you to ease yourself and will help you to get better than before. You may start with the walking. Go for one or two rounds per day. Do not fasten the process at the initial stage as you may feel tiresome. Ensure that you consult your physician.

Deep breathing is great for the beginners. Try it for 3 to 5 minutes each day. Fancy a scene that you have turned down the cigarette offered by someone.

If you are comfortable quitting all of them rapidly then go for it otherwise does it other way round. Plan number of cigarettes you will have each day until your auspicious day. Try to curtail its number each day. Keep changing your brands. This way you will stop enjoying smoking.

Search for companion. Motivate each other. Feel pride in your clean teeth that is not possible with going with the habit of smoking.

Plan your journey to the auspicious day in a different manner. After having completed the passage to two weeks of being a non-smoker, plan to see a movie. After continuing the battle for one month visits a restaurant and so on.

Drink plenty of water every day. It will help to flush all harmful chemicals out of your body. In addition, it helps to reduce your longings for cigarettes.

Try to work pout on the reasons that forces you for a pack of cigarette like work load. Avoid these. Keep your mouth busy with things like chewing gum.

Keep a miniature of someone who always inspires you to adopt good habits. Think that you are trying to escape smoking for you and for that precious person.

CHAPTER 50- WHY WE CANNOT QUIT SMOKING

We do bad things although we know we should not. Nobody knows why? Actually it is not our folly. It falls under the category of things which are beyond our control.

We all know the remedies to lose weight and to quit smoking like good eating habits, exercise .Yet we cannot help ourselves although we desire it. If we talk about the chain smokers, there are many who control themselves but cannot completely quit the habit. The reason is bad temptations. They do every possible thing to keep themselves away from smoking but there is something which acts like a magnetic force and held them back like two opposites constantly attracting each other.

Let us try to find out the answer:

Can we name out some people who are truly happy and serious about their work? Unfortunately the figure is very less. We live in an aura made of our own where we do not feel need to deal with the major issues. It consists of special things which contribute a lot to distract us. We often forget about our ambitions which once we had nurtured in childhood like becoming a doctor, an artist.

This forgetting results in unhappy, unsuccessful and frustrated individuals. They boil their inner self without knowing their problem and what advertisers do? They take benefits of these fears and fulfill their interests by selling us deceptive happiness.

But what about our true needs?

We are either afraid to fulfill them or we disassociate ourselves from it to such an extent that we never think of them again.

One easy way which we opt to escape the problems is we make bad habits our companion as in case of smokers. If they have some family quarrel then they will take up smoking not because of the nicotine temptation but due to their incapability of resolving the problem. When we come face to face with our problems we feel they want us to pay them attention. The surprising fact is if we really want to give attention to them then only we will feel the need of smoking because we know our 'void'. We can solve our problem by taking following easy steps:

Try to listen to your inner voice.

Meditation is great and will surely help.

One should go for a walk by himself listening to his inner self.

We must check ourselves where we are avoiding our problems and what we instantly need. Method of figuring out is different for everyone's but we should try to work on it and not to give it.

ABOUT THE AUTHOR

Jason Scotts has many interests and has written many books about them. In his books, he talks about each passion how it starts, the process and how you can use it in real life situations.

Throughout the course of his career he has become familiar with the challenges that many people have and has also found quite a number of solutions to not only solve those problems but to keep them from resurfacing in the future.

As he is aware that persons do not really have the time to be deciphering text he writes in a way that is easy for everyone to understand.

Through his text Jason helps the reader to learn new techniques or to perfect old ones. He is focused on educating and informing as the main goal to help those who are seeking answers.